GREAT AMERICAN FILM DIRECTORS

IN PHOTOGRAPHS

EDITED BY

RICHARD KOSZARSKI

DOVER PUBLICATIONS, INC.
NEW YORK

A Book for Eva

PHOTOGRAPHER CREDITS
The numbers are those of the photographs.

Robert Coburn: 106.　　John Miehle: 89.
Faxon Dean: 16.　　Newsday, Long Island: 165.
Alex Kahle: 80, 82.　　Ned Scott: 112.
Irving Lippman: 78, 129, 140.　Oliver Sigurdson: 130.
Bert Longworth: 61.　　Van Pelt: 142.
M. Marigold: 57, 96.　　Scott Welborn: 35.
Hal A. McAlpin: 91.

LENDER CREDITS

Kevin Brownlow: 25.
Museum of Modern Art: 2, 3, 97, 120.
Charles Musser: 1.
Marc Wanamaker/Bison Archives: 4, 21, 38, 42,
69, 85, 102, 107, 121, 139, 156, 189.

Copyright © 1984 by Richard Koszarski.
All rights reserved under Pan American and International Copyright Conventions.

Published in Canada by General Publishing Company, Ltd., 30 Lesmill Road, Don Mills, Toronto, Ontario.
Published in the United Kingdom by Constable and Company, Ltd., 10 Orange Street, London WC2H 7EG.

Great American Film Directors in Photographs is a new work, first published by Dover Publications, Inc., in 1984.

Manufactured in the United States of America
Dover Publications, Inc., 31 East 2nd Street, Mineola, N.Y. 11501

Library of Congress Cataloging in Publication Data
Main entry under title:

Great American film directors in photographs.

Includes index.
1. Moving-picture producers and directors—United States—Portraits.
I. Koszarski, Richard.　II. Title.
PN1998.A2G737　1984　　791.43′0233′0922 [B]　　84-6141
ISBN 0-486-24752-X (pbk.)

FOREWORD

There are several ways to view this album: as a pictorial dictionary of American film directors; as a historical survey of the development of film technology over seventy years; even as a retrospective of Hollywood studio portrait styles. But what first raised my interest in these photographs was a simple question of image. When the studio publicity photographer came around, how did Hollywood's prime image makers want themselves pictured?

It's no secret that directors as diverse as Cecil B. De Mille and Alfred Hitchcock spent considerable energy on their personal publicity, forming an image in the public's mind against which their films were meant to be understood. Others may not have been so formally self-conscious, but personal vanity is no stranger to Hollywood, and even an anonymous hack might spend a few minutes in the press office, approving some candid shots and killing others.

Nearly all of these photographs were taken for promotional purposes, although promoting the director was generally an afterthought, the selling of some film usually being the job at hand. So, unlike most photos of novelists or composers, portraits of film directors tend to be associated with specific productions, tracing a life almost entirely in terms of its works.

Because of this inherent historicity the photos have been arranged chronologically, a method that tends to emphasize the social and technological context within which these men and women operated (a full index, including all identified people in the photos, is provided for easier biographical access).

Some directors are seen working on their most memorable films, but this was not a major selection criterion. Rather, characteristic poses (or unusual ones) and elements of special visual interest were given preference. The captions merely supplement these images and are in no way intended to be either comprehensive or objective.

1

1. A mechanic and engineer, **EDWIN S. PORTER** entered films as a projectionist, running the show at New York's Eden Musee in the 1890s. It was a short step from organizing these brief programs to directing for the Edison Company such landmarks of the early cinema as *Life of an American Fireman* and *The Great Train Robbery,* both released in 1903. **2.** With his cameraman Billy Bitzer behind the Pathe, **D. W. GRIFFITH** directs Henry B. Walthall in *Death's Marathon* (1913), one of his last short films for the Biograph Company. Griffith helped create a new narrative structure for the movies while working on hundreds of these shorts, and capped his efforts a few years later with films like *The Birth of a Nation* and *Intolerance.*

2

3. Commodore **J. STUART BLACKTON** was co-founder of the American Vitagraph Company, a pioneer in all aspects of motion picture art and industry. A major contributor to early narrative, documentary, animation and feature production, Blackton was one of the most versatile early filmmakers. He explains the workings of the Vitagraph camera to actor E. H. Sothern in 1916.   **4.** A director who soon turned to producing as a means of extending personal control over a larger number of films, **THOMAS H. INCE** had a few things to say on the set of *Civilization* (1916), a picture nominally directed by Irvin Willat. Ince formalized the Hollywood factory system, leading the way for men like Thalberg and Selznick.

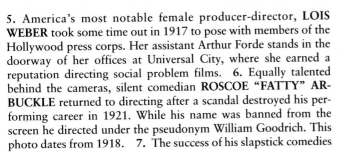

5. America's most notable female producer-director, **LOIS WEBER** took some time out in 1917 to pose with members of the Hollywood press corps. Her assistant Arthur Forde stands in the doorway of her offices at Universal City, where she earned a reputation directing social problem films.   6. Equally talented behind the cameras, silent comedian **ROSCOE "FATTY" AR-BUCKLE** returned to directing after a scandal destroyed his performing career in 1921. While his name was banned from the screen he directed under the pseudonym William Goodrich. This photo dates from 1918.   7. The success of his slapstick comedies won **MACK SENNETT** (right) a place on the prestigious Artcraft distribution program, a distinction he shared in 1918 with Cecil B. De Mille (left) and D. W. Griffith (center). When it came time to take the official photograph his new associates seemed more amused than Hollywood's "King of Comedy."   8. The tremendous expansion of the American film industry at the close of World War I brought many new faces to the movies, including that of director **JOHN STAHL**, seen here at the right, ca.1919. An early specialist in the tearful melodrama, Stahl hit his stride in the 1930s with films like *Back Street* and *Imitation of Life*.

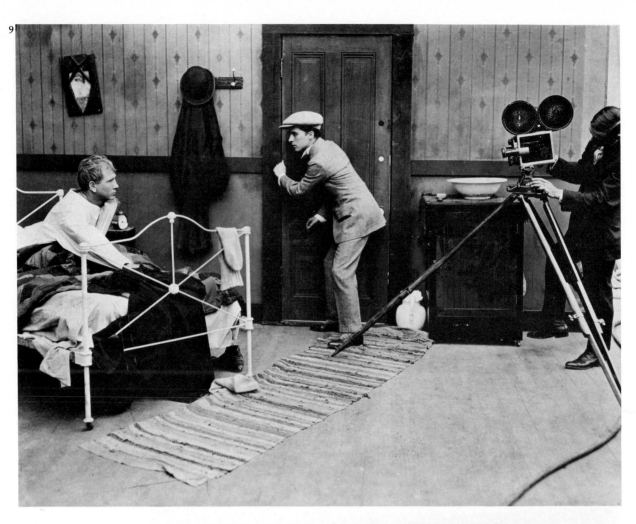

9. Today we remember **CHARLES CHAPLIN** as one of Hollywood's finest, most expressive directors, but audiences of the teens would have been surprised to think of Charlie in those terms. As the screen's top funnyman and one of its greatest stars, the seriousness of his approach to *Sunnyside* (1919) would have puzzled them. Later they learned better. (Tom Wilson is the actor in bed.)   **10.** Noted for his skillful literary adaptations and tremendous pictorial sense, **MAURICE TOURNEUR** was the finest of many émigré French directors in the early American cinema. On the set of *Treasure Island* (1920) he poses with a toothsome Lon Chaney, while Shirley Mason (as Jim) takes time off from an ice cream cone.   **11.** Long overlooked by historians, **REGINALD BARKER** is winning new attention today for the dramatic and emotional complexities of his films for Hart, Ince and many others. Here he poses with Barbara Castleton and cameraman Percy Hilburn on location for *The Branding Iron* (1920).   **12. WILLIAM DESMOND TAYLOR** explains an obscure harem instrument to May McAvoy during the production of *Morals* in 1921. His sensational murder the following year capped a series of Hollywood scandals which traumatized the industry.

13. **CECIL B. DE MILLE** could take justifiable pride at Paramount week in 1921, since he was largely responsible for putting that studio in a position of industry supremacy. Ironically, the week proved a black one for Paramount as the Arbuckle scandal broke over the Labor Day weekend.   14. Cecil's less ostentatious older brother, **WILLIAM DE MILLE,** was the critics' darling but lacked a popular touch. He poses here with his entire production unit, including cameraman Guy Wilky (hand on camera) and, at his feet, a single violinist to help his actors achieve the proper mood.

14

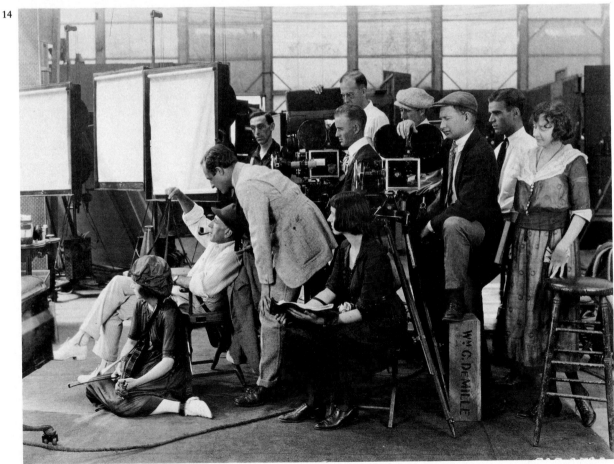

15. SAM WOOD was once an assistant to C. B. De Mille, and spent most of the silent years at Paramount, where he directed all their major stars, including Swanson and Valentino. By the time sound came in he had developed a reputation as a dependable team player, and won assignments like *Goodbye, Mr. Chips* and *King's Row*.   **16. JOSEPH HENABERY** was a disciple of Griffith who spent a lengthy career in B-movies, sponsored films and other fringe areas of the industry. Standing at the far left, he poses with Jack Holt (at table) while filming *Making a Man* on location in Atlantic City (1922).

17. Although his career reached its peak at Warners in the early 1930s, **ALFRED E. GREEN** had a lengthy silent career as well. Here he consults with Thomas Meighan on the script of *The Ne'er Do Well* (1923), filmed on location in the Canal Zone.   **18.** Few directors at the Ince studio were able to exercise much personal control over the films they handled for Mr. Ince, and when he died many of their names faded from film history as well. **JOHN GRIFFITH WRAY** directed some of the best of the late Ince features, notably the original *Anna Christie* (1923), but he, too, failed to survive the studio's demise.   **19.** Best remembered for *The Jazz Singer,* **ALAN CROSLAND** was a skilled silent-era director whose career faded, ironically, with sound. But when he directed Elinor Glyn's *Three Weeks* in 1923 his popularity was substantial, at least among these well-draped extras.   **20.** Thanks to *The Covered Wagon* (1923) **JAMES CRUZE** has a permanent spot in film history. But his reputation for innovative staging of comedies and dramas had already won him the respect of his contemporaries. Sadly, few of his early films survive.

21. REX INGRAM was noted for the rich visual texture of his work, especially such period adventures as *Scaramouche* (1923). Appearing as the young Napoleon in that film was **SLAVKO VORKAPICH,** soon to become Hollywood's chief exponent of "kinesthetics" and montage episodes. (Robespierre, right, was played by DeGarcia Fuerburg.) **22. VICTOR SCHERTZINGER** was originally a concert violinist and theater orchestra conductor, which perhaps explains his interest in Eva and Jane Novak's musical efforts. Many of Schertzinger's pictures had musical subjects, although *The Man Life Passed By* (1924) was not among them. **23.** A pioneer director who had traveled around the world making films for the Kalem Company before World War I, **SIDNEY OLCOTT** was never much at home in Hollywood, and made most of his films in the East. While shooting Olcott's *The Hummingbird* (1924) at Paramount's Astoria studio, Gloria Swanson kept this private dressing room on the main stage. Edmund Burns (right) and Miss Swanson's musical entourage look on while Olcott instructs his star.

24. One of Hollywood's most spectacular location adventures was the filming of *Ben-Hur* in Italy in 1924. **FRED NIBLO** (right) was sent out by M-G-M to replace Charles Brabin, who had started the picture. Ramon Novarro and Frank Currier seem to have had enough of the raft scene at this point. 25. Later they filmed fantastic adventures like *King Kong* inside the Hollywood studios, but the first screen efforts of **MERIAN C. COOPER** (left) and **ERNEST B. SCHOEDSACK** were pioneering documentaries. During the filming of *Grass* (1924) they loaded their tripod and camera on a solitary pack animal and followed the Bakhtiari migration across Central Asia. 26. A talented director of literary adaptations and exceptionally good with actresses, **HERBERT BRENON** poses with Anna Q. Nilsson during production of *The Side Show of Life* (1924). Ernest Torrence played a World War I British officer in this film, which was partially shot at St. Paul's Academy in Garden City, Long Island. Brenon's cameraman, James Wong Howe, stands behind them. 27. The creator of such bizarre classics as *Dracula* and *Freaks,* **TOD BROWNING** earned his reputation in a series of silent films with Lon Chaney. On the set of *The Unholy Three* (1925) Browning stands by the camera while Chaney demonstrates his characterization of the old bird-shop proprietress.

28

29

28. **ROBERT Z. LEONARD,** whose career in films dated back to the nickelodeon era, was for many years a work-horse director at M-G-M. During the shooting of *Cheaper to Marry* in 1925 he stops for a musical moment with Paulette Duval, Conrad Nagel, Marguerite de la Motte and Lewis Stone. 29. **IRVIN WILLAT** was noted for his work in a wide range of adventure genres, including westerns and aviation pictures. For *Airmail* (1925) he demonstrates the function of the telephoto lens to cast members Douglas Fairbanks Jr., Warner Baxter and Billie Dove. 30. Remembered today for his crisp direction of action pictures and nostalgic melodramas, **RAOUL WALSH** was once identified with such exotic costume epics as *The Thief of Bagdad* and *Carmen*. Here, on *East of Suez* (1925), he examines an oriental prop with the actor Sojin. 31. This rare shot of **JOSEF VON STERNBERG** documents a film which the young director barely started. After two weeks of filming Mae Murray in *The Masked Bride* (1925) he ordered the cameras turned to the rafters and walked out of the studio. Miss Murray had that effect on several directors.

32. Rudolph Valentino's last screen appearance was in *Son of the Sheik* (1926), an elegant production directed by the underrated **GEORGE FITZMAURICE**. Trained in Paris as a graphic artist, Fitzmaurice felt that movies were primarily a visual art form, and operated accordingly. Vilma Banky co-starred for him here. **33. ERICH VON STROHEIM** was noted for his obsessive attention to detail, especially as regards uniforms and decorations. On *The Wedding March* (filmed in 1926) he seems to have found a flaw in the work of his military adviser, Captain Albert Conti. Shooting will now be held up until the proper decoration is available. **34.** The name of **PAUL BERN** is usually encountered only once in film histories, in accounts of his marriage to Jean Harlow and his mysterious suicide. But Bern was a talented filmmaker in the Lubitsch tradition who directed such accomplished comedies as *Open All Night*. **35. WILLIAM K. HOWARD** was one of Hollywood's independent spirits, the director of a string of eccentric pictures which did not always please audiences or critics. Here he provides Vera Reynolds with some added ammunition for *The Main Event* (1927).

36. This moody setting was characteristic of *7th Heaven* (1927), the classic romance for which **FRANK BORZAGE** won the first Academy Award for direction. Charlie Farrell and Janet Gaynor are in the cab.   37. **PAUL LENI** was imported from Berlin to design theatrical prologues for Universal's theater chain, but he soon found a place behind the cameras as well. On the set of *The Last Warning* (1928) he jokes with cameraman Hal Mohr and his assistant, Stanley Cortez (in white shirt).   38. Imported by M-G-M along with his protégée, Greta Garbo, **MAURITZ STILLER** was never quite comfortable in Hollywood. Here the contrast between his three-piece suit and the casual whites of the rest of the crew is only too obvious. The film was *The Woman on Trial* (1927), one of the few he was able to complete in America.   39. **DOROTHY ARZNER** moved from editing to directing, and became one of Paramount's busiest directors in the late 1920s. Here she lines up a shot with her handy viewfinder-megaphone for *Get Your Man* (1927), a bright little Clara Bow comedy. Alfred Gilks is at the camera.

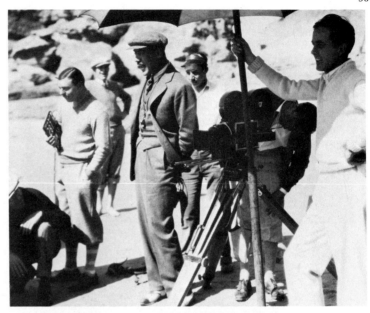

39

40. **BUSTER KEATON,** the most technically accomplished of the screen's master comedians, was able to draw humor from a host of mechanical contrivances, from steamships to railway engines. The movie camera itself was often a favorite target, as in his last great film, *The Cameraman* (1928), in which his hero tries to become a stringer for the M-G-M newsreel. Harold Goodwin is at the left. **41.** A research scientist whose interest in theater and film got the better of him in the 1920s, **PAUL FEJOS** was for a time the top director at Universal. Mary Philbin starred in his *The Last* *Performance* (1928) and Hal Mohr (looking through camera) handled the bizarre photography. Fejos later turned to documentaries, and eventually abandoned films altogether for scientific research. **42.** Unlike his compatriot Stiller, **VICTOR SEASTROM** (Sjöström) was not afraid to roll up his sleeves when the need arose, and his American career was considerably more fruitful. The large aluminum reflector provides a lightweight source of fill light for this moving shot from *The Divine Woman* (1928).

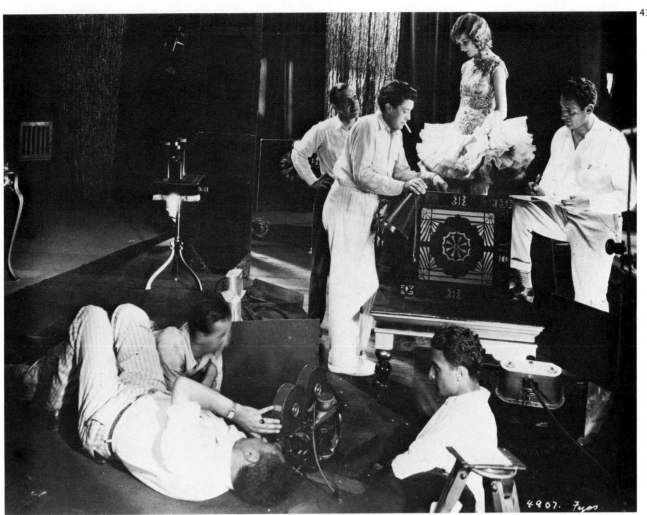

43

44

43. MAL ST. CLAIR learned comedy direction from Sennett, Keaton and Chaplin, but his own best films recall the elegant drawing-room style of Ernst Lubitsch. One of his greatest successes was the original *Gentlemen Prefer Blondes* (1928) with Ruth Taylor as Lorelei Lee. **44. ROWLAND V. LEE** was a sensitive director whose work is only now winning adequate attention. Here he rehearses Florence Vidor for an emotional sequence in *Doomsday* (1928), one of his last silent films. **45.** Lupe Velez was **VICTOR FLEMING**'s star in *Wolf Song* (1929), one of Paramount's first talkies. But Fleming's best years were at M-G-M,

where he directed such exotic adventure films as *Red Dust* and *Treasure Island*. When George Cukor was removed from *Gone With the Wind* it was Fleming who was called in to finish the picture. **46.** Directors of talkies needed ears as well as eyes. **EDDIE SUTHERLAND** (left) and **JOHN CROMWELL** (right) used these headsets to monitor sound levels on *The Dance of Life* (1929). As was the habit at the time, the film employed two directors, Broadway import Cromwell for the dialogue and Hollywood veteran Sutherland for the rest. J. Roy Hunt still managed the camera all by himself.

47

48

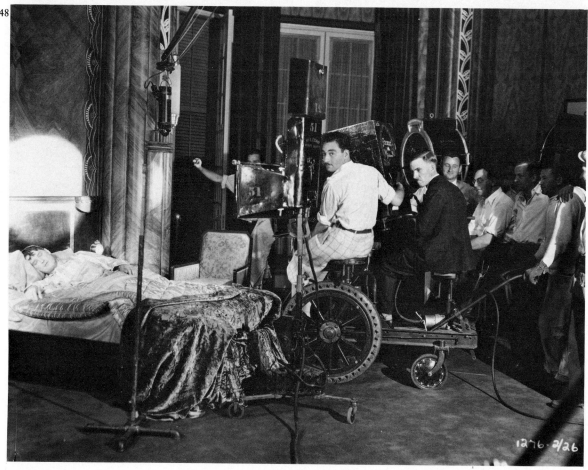

47. The man lining up the shot could only be **BUSBY BERKELEY,** dance director on Sam Goldwyn's *Whoopee!* (1930). Standing by is the film's official director, **THORNTON FREELAND.** Here Berkeley introduced the overhead shots and other tricks of camera choreography which he would develop more fully at Warners a few years later. Freeland, who also knew a bit about musicals, later directed *Flying Down to Rio.* **48.** Sound temporarily paralyzed the camera, but it began to move again as soon as silencing "blimps" were introduced to quiet the grinding of its gears. Here German director **LUDWIG BERGER** rides the dolly on *Playboy of Paris* (1930), one of the early Maurice Chevalier vehicles. **49.** According to the original caption, this tableau shows the creators of *All Quiet on the Western Front* (1930) doing "some deep thinking" during a scripting session. Scenarist Dell Andrews, director **LEWIS MILESTONE** and dialogue writer Maxwell Anderson appear to be doing most of the thinking, while **GEORGE CUKOR,** imported from New York to work as dialogue director, leafs through the research photos. **50.** One of Chaplin's most gifted collaborators, **MONTA BELL** directed a string of enjoyable light comedies in the 1920s and early 30s, then turned to producing. On *Young Man of Manhattan* (1930) he gave a break to Ginger Rogers; that piece of the statue in her hand is a telephone.

51. Like his rival Mack Sennett, whom he had supplanted by the 1920s, **HAL ROACH** moved quickly from directing to producing. The developer of Harold Lloyd, Our Gang and the Laurel and Hardy team, Roach probably found ready use for this truckload of trophies.   **52. GEORGE ABBOTT** brought his considerable stage experience to bear on such early talkies as *My Sin* (1931), a melodramatic Tallulah Bankhead vehicle. But his screen career never matched the importance of his stage career, which was studded with classics like *Broadway* and *Pal Joey*.   **53.** This photograph of the great German director **F. W. MURNAU** is one of the last formal portraits taken before his death in 1931. Paramount had just agreed to distribute his South Sea picture *Tabu,* which he had made independently with Robert Flaherty, but Murnau never lived to see the release.   **54.** Long associated with Buster Keaton, **EDDIE CLINE** (left) was also responsible for such classic comedies as *Million Dollar Legs* and *The Bank Dick*. Here he directs Charlie Ruggles in *The Girl Habit,* made at the Paramount Astoria studio in 1931.

55. A notable director of child stars, **NORMAN TAUROG** made his reputation with films like *Skippy, Boys Town* and *Young Tom Edison*. Here he waits with Mitzi Green while the crew lights the next scene of *Forbidden Adventure* (1931).   56. Two Viennese émigrés pose in the rain during the shooting of *The Wiser Sex* (1932). Famed stage director **BERTHOLD VIERTEL** (with mittens) was directing the picture, while his assistant **FRED ZINNEMANN** (in light coat) would have to wait a few years before becoming a director himself. Cameramen George Folsey and Joe Ruttenberg stand at left.   57. **JAMES PARROTT** is representative of so many directors who excelled in shorts, but never had much of a chance with features. Noted for his fine work with Laurel and Hardy (*Pardon Us* was one of his few long pictures), Parrott also made many films with his brother, Charlie Chase, about to take a dip here in *Girl Grief* (1932).   58. Theatre Guild director **ROUBEN MAMOULIAN** made some of the finest early talkies, notably *Applause* and *Love Me Tonight* (1932). His parents came to visit him on the set of the latter, a landmark musical for which that conductor's baton was especially useful.

56

PGP-21282

59. A director of taste and distinction, **CLARENCE BROWN** was equally at home with "Americana" subjects like *The Yearling* or sophisticated high-society melodramas like *Letty Lynton* (1932). Robert Montgomery and Joan Crawford share his table.   **60. CHARLES BRABIN**, an industry pioneer, was reduced to directing B's for M-G-M during the first years of sound, but *The Mask of Fu Manchu* (1932) showed he had no problems with the new medium.

Veteran cameraman Tony Gaudio stands behind Brabin, while Boris Karloff prepares to look oriental.   **61.** The success of *42nd Street* (1933) was due as much to **LLOYD BACON**'s sensitive handling of the film's backstage plot as to Busby Berkeley's work on the musical numbers. Here Bacon sits back as the show's "director," Warner Baxter, takes the chorus through its paces. Bebe Daniels and George E. Stone are in the orchestra.

P868-1

62. This smiling portrait shows the young **HENRY HATHAWAY,** well pleased with himself since Paramount has just promoted him to director. Hathaway's first films were B-westerns, but that didn't mean he couldn't dress up a little.   **63.** Was **LEO McCAREY** the greatest director of comedy? He certainly seems to have had the widest range of success, from the screwball classic *The Awful Truth* to the more physical antics of Laurel and Hardy and W. C. Fields. Groucho and Chico Marx seem to have slowed him down a bit on *Duck Soup* (1933), at least until Groucho finishes the script.

63

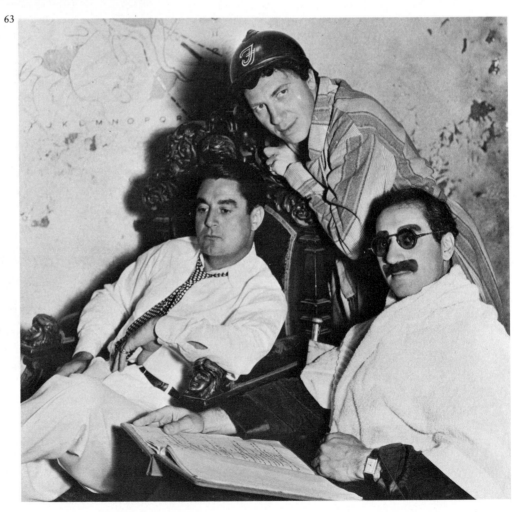

64. Many directors seemed to favor this pose, seated at the ready beneath their cameras, and generally feigned enthusiasm, seriousness or some vaguely artistic quality. What **ALFRED WERKER** is trying to express here is unclear, but the director of *The Adventures of Sherlock Holmes* and many other bread-and-butter assignments was seldom noted for introspection. Taken on the set of Paramount's *You Belong to Me* (1934).   65. Once an assistant to D. W. Griffith, **W. S. VAN DYKE** soon acquired the nickname "One Shot Woody" because of the speed at which he directed pictures like *The Thin Man* (1934). William Powell looks on while James Wong Howe mans the camera.

66. Colbert and Gable were not impressed with the script for "Night Bus," but **FRANK CAPRA** (right) turned it into one of his greatest hits, *It Happened One Night* (1934). Visiting at left is Colbert's husband, **NORMAN FOSTER,** soon to begin a lengthy career directing programmers for Fox and Disney.   67. **KING VIDOR** was one great director who had little trouble turning the M-G-M colossus to his own ends. In films as diverse as *The Big Parade, The Crowd* and *Northwest Passage*, he used that studio's facilities to help express a highly personal vision of the American character and landscape. This portrait dates from the time of his one major break with the studio system, his production of *Our Daily Bread* in 1934.   68. The tired man in the wheelchair is **MARSHALL NEILAN,** once one of Hollywood's boy wonders and Mary Pickford's favorite director. Working with Helen Mack and Joe E. Brown in *The Lemon Drop Kid* (1934) seems to have been too much for him; it proved to be one of his last films.

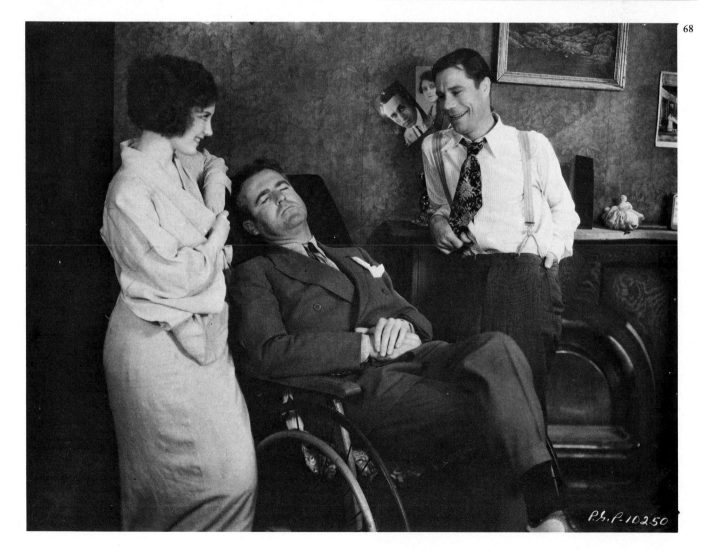

P.S.P-10250

69

69. Cameraman Hal Mohr and director **HENRY KING** study the dailies over breakfast during the shooting of *Carolina* in 1934. A poet of the American landscape, King was unmatched for his handling of small-town life, especially in such classics as *Tol'able David*, *Stella Dallas* and *Margie*.   **70. JEAN NEGULESCO** was a Roumanian stage director whose first work in Hollywood was as a second-unit or associate director on films like *Kiss and Make Up* (1934). His most prolific years were at Fox in the early 1950s where he handled many of the first CinemaScope films, including *How to Marry a Millionaire* and *Three Coins in the Fountain*.

70

71. CHRISTY CABANNE was the quintessential B-movie director. Trained by Griffith, he spent most of his lengthy career spinning out supporting features for Universal, RKO or worse. Here he is at Monogram in 1935 on the aptly titled *The Keeper of the Bees,* with Neil Hamilton and Betty Furness.   **72. NORMAN McLEOD,** whose best films were comedies like *Horse Feathers* and *Topper,* was originally a cartoonist and illustrator. On the set of *Here Comes Cookie* (1935), a Burns and Allen picture, he is seen working on a new comic strip he has created called "Slim Pickens."

73. **HOWARD HAWKS** (left) and cameraman Gregg Toland did not work on *Come and Get It* (1935) very long, for Samuel Goldwyn replaced both of them. But they did stay long enough to pose for this shot with their star, the controversial Frances Farmer. Hawks continued his astonishing series of thoughtful action pictures, which included *Scarface, The Big Sleep* and *Red River*. 74. **WESLEY RUGGLES** was an old-time director who is best remembered today for some of his early sound films, notably *Cimarron* and *Bolero*. On *The Bride Comes Home* (1935) he presented his star, Claudette Colbert, with a Friday-the-Thirteenth birthday cake. Claudette's mother waits for her piece at right. 75. This rare shot shows **LOWELL SHERMAN** (facing Miriam Hopkins) directing the first full-Technicolor feature, *Becky Sharp* (1935). Sherman, who is better remembered as the villain in Griffith's *Way Down East,* directed a string of literate programmers for RKO and other studios in the early 1930s. His work on *Becky Sharp* was cut short when he died two weeks into production. 76. **FRANK TUTTLE** was a Paramount house director whose career at that studio spanned over twenty years. Eddie Cantor's *Kid Boots* and Alan Ladd's *This Gun for Hire* were two of his most successful films, but *All the King's Horses* (1935), with Carl Brisson, is more typical of his usual assignments.

74

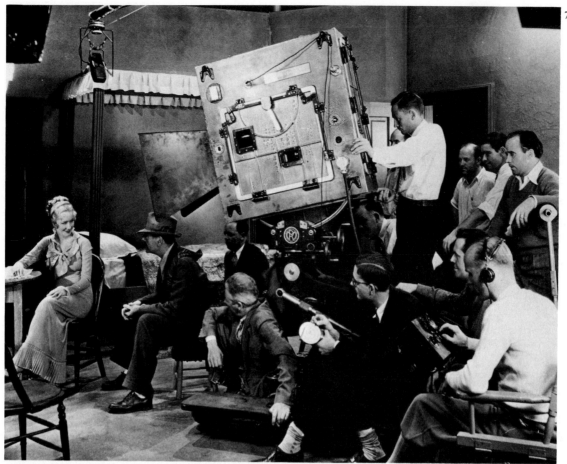

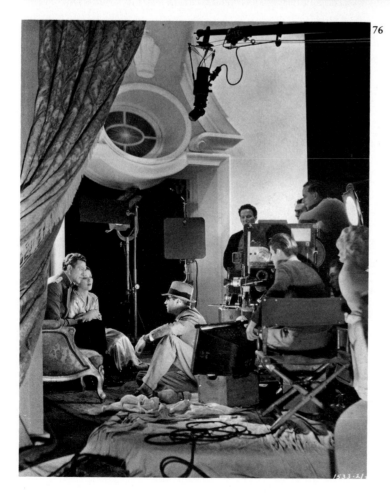

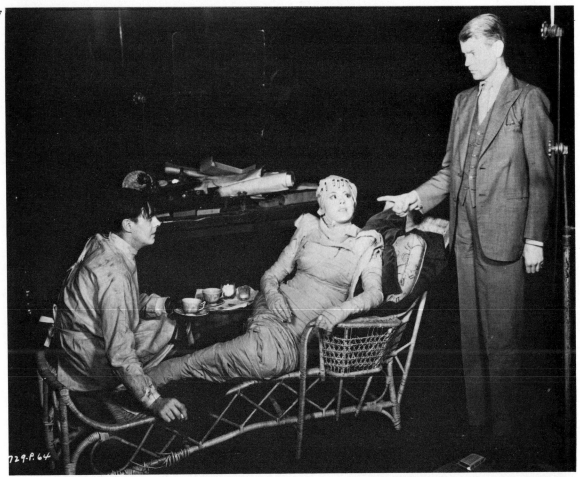

77. Hollywood's British colony hasn't received the attention offered the other immigrant groups, but it was especially rich in writing and acting talent. **JAMES WHALE** was one of the first to achieve directing success, most notably with his series of classic horror films at Universal. Custom dictates a tea break here for Colin Clive, Elsa Lanchester and director Whale on the set of *The Bride of Frankenstein* (1935). 78. **RICHARD BOLESLAWSKY** came to Hollywood from Warsaw, by way of the Moscow Art Theatre. In America his stage work ranged from Reinhardt to Ziegfeld, and he entered films as a director of musical sequences. Boleslawsky reclines under the camera while cinematographer Joseph Walker (in white hat) prepares to shoot Melvyn Douglas and Irene Dunne for *Theodora Goes Wild* (1936). 79. The first major Hollywood screenwriters to win the right to direct their own scripts, **BEN HECHT** (left) and **CHARLES MacARTHUR** had to go east for the honor. Here they discuss a fine point of interpretation at Paramount's Astoria studio while Mary Taylor and Lionel Stander (in car) wait to get back to work on *Soak the Rich* (1936). 80. When not directing westerns, **JOHN FORD** tried his hand at a range of genres, including an occasional literary adaptation. Cameraman Joe August gives some advice to an uncertain Fredric March on *Mary of Scotland* (1936), while Ford sucks on his own pipe at left.

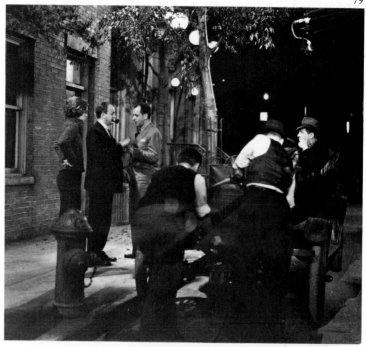

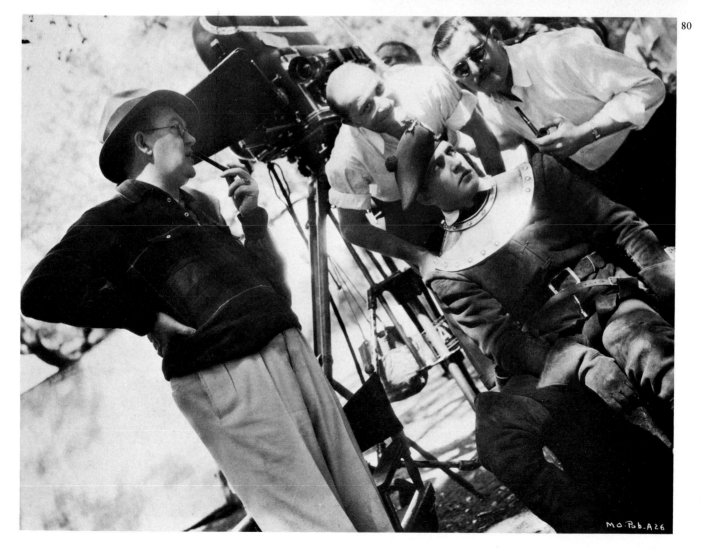

MO-Pub-A26

81. **E. A. DUPONT**'s *Variety* was the one German film that had the greatest impact on American audiences, but Dupont was unable to recapture its success in later years either in Hollywood or Europe. *A Night of Mystery* (1936) was a Paramount programmer, just a cut above the low-budget quickies that ended his career in the 1950s. 82. According to the original caption, **ANATOLE LITVAK** was the "famous Russian director from France." The somewhat puzzling tag does seem to fit, as Litvak's career moved from one capital to another in true international style. Here Litvak directs Miriam Hopkins in his first American film, *The Woman I Love* (1937); they later married. (Elizabeth Risdon is in the center.)

82

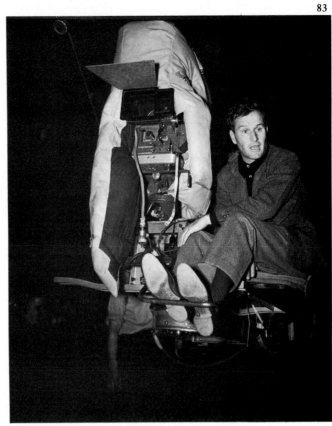

83. World War I air ace **WILLIAM WELLMAN** was noted for such aviation epics as *Wings,* but he could take to the air on an oversized camera crane as well. Here Wellman swings into action on *A Star Is Born* (1937), the original Janet Gaynor version and one of his greatest successes.   **84.** An often bemused observer of the Hollywood scene, **ROBERT FLOREY** was an efficient and sometimes stylish director, as well as a memoirist of rare ability. On the set of *Mountain Music* (1937) he seems to be making a note of Martha Raye for future reference.

84

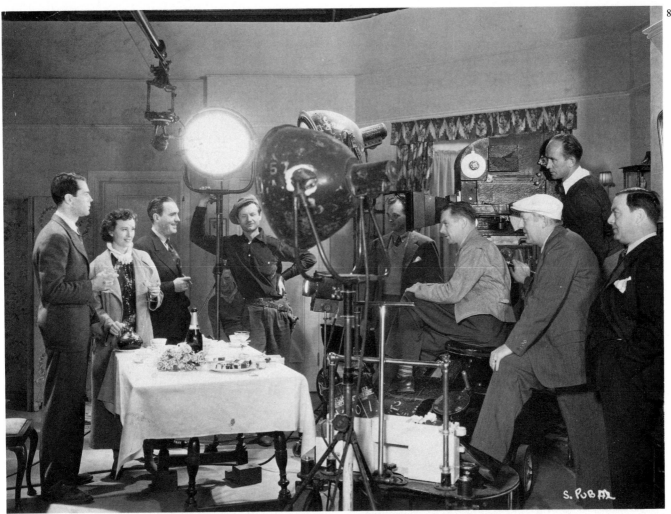

S. PUBAL

85. A veteran whose career began with the "Flying A" company in the days of one-reelers, **ALLAN DWAN** had one of the richest and most varied careers of anyone in Hollywood. Among other accomplishments he directed some of Shirley Temple's best films, including *Heidi* (1937).   86. He entered films as an actor in 1909, but **IRVING CUMMINGS** soon switched to directing, and during many years at Fox produced an enjoyable string of melodramas and musicals. *Merry-Go-Round of 1938* (1937) was a loan-out to Universal photographed by Joe Valentine (at left) and featuring comedians Bert Lahr, Billy House, Mischa Auer and Jimmy Savo.   87. **RAY ENRIGHT** was one of those nearly anonymous craftsmen who passed through the Warner Bros. sweatshop in the 1930s, part of the group who took over when Mervyn LeRoy or Michael Curtiz were busy. Here Enright (seated on camera) directs Henry Fonda, Margaret Lindsay and Pat O'Brien in *Slim* (1937).   88. Megaphones remained in use well into the sound period for crowd scenes and other less intimate events. Normally a successful drawing-room director, **SIDNEY FRANKLIN** used one to shout out his orders on *The Good Earth* (1937), producer Irving Thalberg's last film.

89. A fixture at RKO in the 1930s, **MARK SANDRICH** directed five of the Astaire-Rogers musicals, including *Carefree* (1938). Sandrich worked himself up the hard way, spending the silent years as a gag man and assistant director before finding a series of short comedies to direct. Fred, Ginger, Luella Gear and Ralph Bellamy at left. 90. **FRITZ LANG** came to epitomize the new breed of "German" director in Hollywood, and was the first since von Stroheim to handle a monocle properly (although both, in fact, were Austrian). Here Lang works with Warren Hymer on the script of *You and Me* (1938), a strange musical drama scored by Kurt Weill that starred Sylvia Sidney and George Raft.

91

91. FRANK LLOYD was a prolific silent director whose talkie career was less active, if more influential. Best remembered for *Mutiny on the Bounty,* Lloyd was afloat again with *Rulers of the Sea* (1938), for which he also served as producer.   **92.** A director noted for his westerns, adventure pictures and broad comedies, **GEORGE MARSHALL** (center) scored an unexpected success in 1939 with *Destry Rides Again.* Marlene Dietrich, who was being cast against type in an effort to save her flagging career, cools her heels as Marshall explains the next set-up.

92

1083-P/02.

93. Like Hitchcock, director **TAY GARNETT** also made a habit of appearing in his own films. For *Seven Sinners* (1940) he played a drunk in a South Seas dive. Marlene Dietrich checks him out in the role just before shooting.　**94.** A fictional creation of W. C. Fields's, **A. PISMO CLAM** was often carried to the set by a team of loyal grips, and affected a fondness for the rocking director's chair. This shot from *The Bank Dick* (1940) shows Clam (played by Jack Norton) still using the oversized megaphone of silent days.　**95.** Just before World War II the young **GARSON KANIN** directed a string of hits for RKO, including the witty Irene Dunne vehicle *My Favorite Wife* (1940). After working on government films for the duration, Kanin turned to screenwriting, and with his wife Ruth Gordon wrote some of the best of the Tracy and Hepburn classics.

96. After a series of Tom Mix silents, **LEWIS SEILER** (left) graduated to secondary features at Warners and other studios. *It All Came True* (1940) was not atypical; Jeffrey Lynn and Ann Sheridan provided the love interest, and Ernest Haller (center) was cinematographer. **97.** When RKO imported the young **ORSON WELLES** from New York they gave him near autonomy in the production of his first film. But neither that studio nor anyone in Hollywood could have predicted the explosive originality of *Citizen Kane* (1941). Welles stands by the camera while cinematographer Gregg Toland is just visible on the ground at right. **98. ALFRED HITCHCOCK** was imported by David O. Selznick on the strength of his high-style thrillers and melodramas, yet once in Hollywood a new level of sophistication soon became apparent in his work. Here is Hitchcock with two of his favorite performers, Cary Grant and Joan Fontaine, during the shooting of *Suspicion* (1941). **99.** Hollywood filled up with refugee directors during the war, but not all of them were able to adapt their style to conditions in America. **JULIEN DUVIVIER,** in dark shirt, did his best with films like *Lydia* (1941), featuring Merle Oberon and Joseph Cotten. Leaning his elbow on the camera is cinematographer Lee Garmes.

100. **PRESTON STURGES** was not only a master of comedy, but a pioneer in the movement of screenwriters into directing. On *Sullivan's Travels* (1941) he filled both roles himself, but even so the usual hostility between writer and director continued unabated. 101. Producer-director **GEORGE STEVENS**, here working on *The More the Merrier* (1942) at Columbia, took special pains with the photography of his films, having been a cameraman earlier in his career. While working for Hal Roach he shot many of the best Laurel and Hardy two-reelers, odd preparation indeed for such later Stevens classics as *A Place in the Sun* and *Giant*. 102. German import **CURTIS BERNHARDT** (left) was noted for his psychological thrillers for Warner Bros., so *Happy Go Lucky* (1942) was a real change of pace. Bernhardt lines up the Technicolor camera on Mary Martin as cinematographer Karl Struss watches at right.

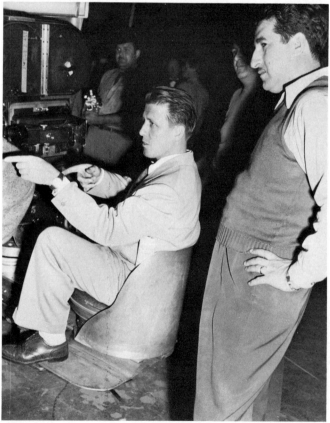

101

102

103. Prolific director of B-westerns, B-musicals and low-budget thrillers, **AL ROGELL** moved quickly into television when that medium usurped the inexpensive feature format. *True to the Army* (1942) was one of a series of wartime Ann Miller musicals for Paramount. Here Rogell is held at bay by Judy Canova.   104. A longtime comedy specialist, ex-cartoonist **GREGORY LA CAVA** directed some of W. C. Fields's first and best pictures, as well as such landmark screwball comedies as *My Man Godfrey*. *Lady in a Jam* (1942) was a late entry in the screwball cycle, and one of La Cava's last films; Irene Dunne starred, with Ralph Bellamy as the singing cowboy.

105

106

105. JACK CONWAY was one of M-G-M's old reliables, a dependable veteran familiar with every aspect of the industry, and a special favorite of Louis B. Mayer. With William Powell looking over his shoulder, Conway critiques a set of models and sketches offered him by the *Crossroads* art department (1942). **106.** *To Be or Not to Be* (1942) was **ERNST LUBITSCH**'s most demanding production, and certainly his most controversial: a black comedy on the occupation of Warsaw in World War II. Jack Benny prepares to go into the title soliloquy, but Lubitsch is more concerned with directing the audience reaction. **107.** According to Hollywood legend, the script of *Casablanca* (1943) was coming off the typewriter just one step ahead of director **MICHAEL CURTIZ**'s shooting schedule. With some fresh pages to work with, Humphrey Bogart and Ingrid Bergman join Curtiz for a quick run-through of the day's work. **108.** One of M-G-M's most ingenious directors of musicals, **GEORGE SIDNEY** peers over the Technicolor camera during a musical sequence for *Bathing Beauty* (1944). Sidney's great musicals, like *Anchors Aweigh* and *The Harvey Girls,* would come later. Ethel Smith is at the organ.

109. The director of a series of delicate fantasies in Europe and America, **RENÉ CLAIR** tried to capture that rare mood again in *It Happened Tomorrow* (1944). Cinematographer Archie Stout is paying attention, but the stills cameraman seems to think that this is going to be one of those UFA productions. **110.** A refugee whose American career was limited to a brief ten years, **ROBERT SIODMAK** made most of his pictures in Germany and France. While in Hollywood he was notably successful with a string of *film noir* thrillers, including *The Killers, Criss Cross* and *The Suspect* (1945), with Ella Raines. **111.** Originally an actor and director who came to Hollywood to make "German versions" of early talkies, **WILLIAM DIETERLE** proved one of the most adaptable of all the émigrés. From Paul Muni biographies at Warners he moved easily to a series of schmaltzy romances for David O. Selznick, including *I'll Be Seeing You* (1944) with Ginger Rogers.

112. Born in Budapest, **CHARLES VIDOR** received his film training in Germany, and came to Hollywood in 1924. His best-remembered films were produced at Columbia during the war, including *Cover Girl, Gilda* and *A Song to Remember* (1945), with Cornel Wilde as Chopin and Merle Oberon as George Sand.   **113. MITCHELL LEISEN** first made a reputation as Cecil B. De Mille's art director, and in 1932 became one of the few to move from designing pictures to directing them. He spent nearly his entire career at Paramount, where his films were always noted for the elegance of their decor. This studied pose is from *Masquerade in Mexico* (1945).   **114.** Among the gadgets in **WALT DISNEY**'s office was the praxinoscope, a nineteenth-century optical toy that gave life to a strip of cartoon illustrations. Disney was able to turn this instant of repeated motion into the grand narrative flow of the feature-length cartoon, a genre in which he had few competitors. A publicity shot taken during the filming of *The Three Caballeros* (1945).   **115.** The best-known of the wartime refugees, **JEAN RENOIR** calls for action on location for *The Southerner* (1945). Renoir was able to direct several successful Hollywood films, but he chafed at the restrictions of the American studio system, where the need for organization allowed little room for experiment and spontaneity.

114

115

116. Directors occasionally had to pose for "human interest" pictures like this, which were usually targeted for fan-magazine spreads. Here, in 1946, **RICHARD WALLACE**, a generally uninspired contract director of the 1930s and 40s, demonstrates his hobby of model-airplane construction. 117. Another Warners veteran, **ARCHIE MAYO** spent a busy decade there handling everything from the sentimental *Sonny Boy* to the stark *Black Legion*. He left in 1937 to seek his fortune with Goldwyn and Fox, but never

seemed to find the proper material. *Angel on My Shoulder* (1946) with Anne Baxter was his last film.   118. An actor, director and composer, **EDMUND GOULDING** (in dark suit) was one of Hollywood's smoothest professionals, the director of such luxurious star vehicles as *Grand Hotel* and *Dark Victory*. *The Razor's Edge* (1946) proved to be one of his most popular, an entertaining pastiche of philosophy and melodrama which starred an unlikely Tyrone Power, here shading his eyes at the chessboard.

119. ARCH OBOLER came to films from radio, where he made his reputation on the classic "Lights Out!" His initial contract with M-G-M was undistinguished, *The Arnelo Affair* (1946) with Frances Gifford and John Hodiak being typical. But Oboler electrified the nation a few years later with the first NaturalVision 3-D feature, *Bwana Devil*. **120.** With such masterworks as *Nanook of the North* and *Moana*, **ROBERT FLAHERTY** pioneered in the development of screen documentary. More comfortable in the field than in the editing room, Flaherty often allowed free rein to the cutters who gave dramatic form to his material. Here he makes a rare visit to Helen Van Dongen's editing bench during the production of *Louisiana Story* (1948). **121.** At the close of World War II many directors left the sound stages and went out on location, making New York or San Francisco important characters in the postwar cinema. **JACQUES TOURNEUR** (with glasses) traveled all the way to Germany for *Berlin Express* (1947), a stylish thriller featuring Paul Lukas and Merle Oberon, at right. **122. ELLIOTT NUGENT**, an experienced theater professional who entered films as an actor, was most successful with such literate properties as *Three Cornered Moon* and *The Male Animal*. The set model here represents Akim Tamiroff's tie factory in *My Girl Tisa* (1948), an immigrant saga which starred Lilli Palmer.

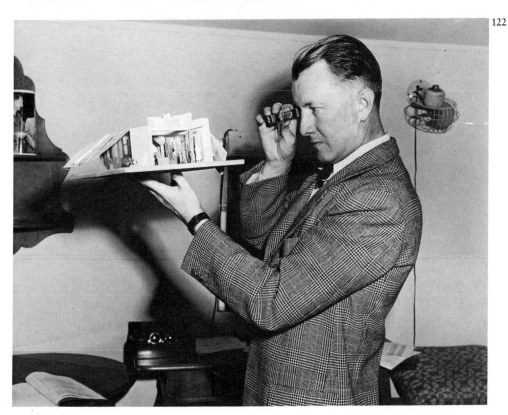

123

123. **MERVYN LeROY** demonstrates that the director needs to pay personal attention to every detail of production. For designer Walter Plunkett's benefit he indicates the proper spot for a patch in June Allyson's gown on the set of *Little Women* (1948), which LeRoy produced and directed at the peak of his power at M-G-M. 124. **MAX OPHULS,** on director's stool, is set to roll along with his camera dolly during the shooting of *Caught* (1949). Cameraman Lee Garmes shouts out an order while James Mason muses at left. "A shot that does not call for tracks/Is agony for poor old Max," wrote Mason later, remembering Ophuls' penchant for camera movement.

124

125. H. BRUCE HUMBERSTONE was a contract director of modest skill who was happiest with a good Charlie Chan script. For the rest of the time he handled musicals, westerns or Tarzan pictures with equanimity. Here he explains his hand-painted tie to Shelley Winters during the production of *South Sea Sinner* (1950). **126.** A pioneer in the postwar exploitation field, director **HUGO HAAS** (in dark jacket) often wrote and acted in his own low-budget melodramas, in addition to producing and directing them. He is offscreen for the moment in this scene from *Pick Up* (1950), while Allan Nixon and Beverly Michaels do their stuff for cameraman Paul Ivano (in beret).

127. BILLY WILDER's *Sunset Boulevard* (1950) was a dark valentine to the silent film, energized by two of the era's most fabulous characters, Gloria Swanson and Erich von Stroheim. Wilder acts as if he has seen this look from von Stroheim before. Was Erich giving his opinion of Gloria's Charlie Chaplin imitation?   **128. IDA LUPINO** was the one woman director active in Hollywood in the postwar period. Forming her own company, she directed a series of inexpensive features, often keyed to women's issues. *Outrage* (1950) was a sensitive drama of the aftermath of a rape, which she co-scripted as well as directed.   **129.** The writer of a series of powerful Warners dramas during the prewar years, **ROBERT ROSSEN** began directing in 1947, but the blacklist soon disrupted his career. *The Brave Bulls* (1951), with Miroslava, was one of the relatively few Hollywood pictures shot on location in Mexico.   **130.** *On Dangerous Ground* (1951) was one of the more offbeat films of **NICHOLAS RAY** (left), whose career was noted for his idiosyncratic handling of standard Hollywood genres. Robert Ryan starred in this strange psychological-romance-cop film, which puzzled the critics even more than Ray's other work.

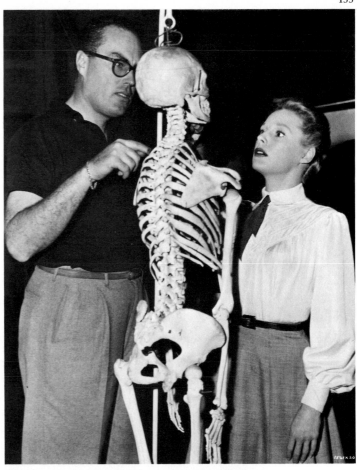

131. David Wayne looks on while **JOSEPH LOSEY** studies his script notes for the remake of the German classic *M* (1951). Losey's interesting Hollywood career was completely aborted by the blacklist era. He picked it up quite successfully in England, where he stayed until his death. 132. The man with the megaphone on his sombrero is **ALBERT LEWIN,** the director of a handful of highly self-conscious films in the late 1940s and early 50s, including *Pandora and the Flying Dutchman* (1951). His partner is Jack Cardiff, perhaps the greatest of color cinematographers, and later a director in his own right. 133. *The Girl in White* (1951) was the story of the first woman doctor in the New York City hospital system. June Allyson was directed by **JOHN STURGES,** who was midway between a career as a wartime documentarian for the Air Force and a new career as the creator of such outsized canvases as *The Magnificent Seven* and *The Great Escape.* 134. **JOSEPH L. MANKIEWICZ** discusses the fine points of *Julius Caesar* (1952) with some of his cast: John Gielgud, Greer Garson and Deborah Kerr. Mankiewicz's own literary talents were better suited to the contemporary idiom of *All About Eve* and *A Letter to Three Wives,* although he did give the bard one of his better Hollywood productions.

135. The task of handling the first CinemaScope picture fell to **HENRY KOSTER**, a German-born director then known mainly for his work with Deanna Durbin. On the set of *The Robe* (1953) Koster works with Caligula (Jay Robinson) while Jean Simmons and part of the cast of thousands wait quietly. 136. The most spectacular movie fad of the 1950s was the 3-D craze, and most successful at the box office was *House of Wax* (1953), by Hungarian actor-director **ANDRE DE TOTH.** While his stars Phyllis Kirk and Vincent Price watch in horror, de Toth seems to be looking at another film; in fact, having only one good eye, he was incapable of seeing any stereo effects. 137. The screen's greatest dancer-director-actor-choreographer, **GENE KELLY,** made *Invitation to the Dance* in 1954, although M-G-M kept the film on the shelf for two more years. When he first began to direct in 1949 Kelly was partnered with Stanley Donen, a three-picture collaboration which produced such classics as *Singin' in the Rain.*

138

139

©D-8271-RP11

138. The director of such classic westerns as *Broken Arrow* and *3:10 to Yuma*, **DELMER DAVES** was as comfortable on location as he was on the back lot. Originally a writer, Daves also scripted many of his best pictures. Here he describes the next sequence of *Jubal* (1955). 139. The use of hand-held shots in the 1940s and 50s provided a new sense of realism, especially for action scenes like this one from *The Harder They Fall* (1955). Cameraman Burnett Guffey (in argyle socks) did the best he could with the limited dolly equipment available, while director **MARK ROBSON** (in dark jacket) took the opportunity to help assist as camera grip. 140. Westerns reached their peak of popularity in the 1950s, thanks largely to the work of directors like **ANTHONY MANN**. After having handled some of the darkest *film noir* thrillers of the 1940s, Mann brought to films like *The Man from Laramie* (1955) an introspective, adult quality. Here he rehearses Arthur Kennedy and Cathy O'Donnell. 141. Like Gregory La Cava and a few others, **FRANK TASHLIN** came to features from a career in comic strips and cartoons. Any audience watching the bright colors and broad, almost surreal situations of his best films finds this easy to believe. *The Lieutenant Wore Skirts* (1955) featured one of Tashlin's brightest blondes, Sheree North.

142

143

144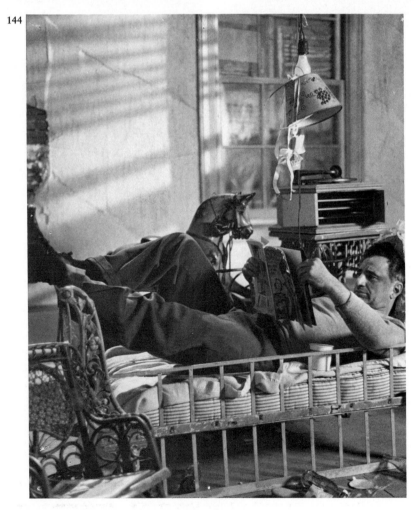

142. One characteristic element of the 1950s crime films was the use of real city locations, and **PHIL KARLSON,** director of *Kansas City Confidential* and *The Phenix City Story,* helped pioneer the genre. For *Five Against the House* (1955) he took Kim Novak and Brian Keith out on location to Reno, Nevada. **143.** Director **DON SIEGEL,** once a montage specialist at Warners, is able to take the most lightweight action genres and create something of intelligence and distinction. Perhaps the best example is *The Invasion of the Body Snatchers* (1956), with Kevin McCarthy and Dana Wynter, the most chilling of 1950s

science-fiction films. **144. ELIA KAZAN** is not killing time on the set, but demonstrating for Carroll Baker just how he wants a certain scene played in *Baby Doll* (1956). The Tennessee Williams work, like many of Kazan's pictures, was filmed not in Hollywood but in newly renovated studios in New York. **145.** Gregory Peck was Ahab in one of the 1950s' most ambitious literary adaptations, *Moby Dick* (1956). Director **JOHN HUSTON,** who had moved up from screenwriting in the early 1940s, gave the film a visual grandeur well suited to the poetry of the original novel.

146

146. *Friendly Persuasion* (1956) was a momentary respite for **WILLIAM WYLER,** who for most of his career was associated with temperamental dramatic stars and inflated budgets. Noted for his conscientious work with actors, Wyler appears to be taking time out to confer with a duck on his part in the next scene. The duck's friends include Dorothy McGuire and Anthony Perkins. **147.** A debut film for **ARTHUR PENN,** *The Left Handed Gun* (1957) was a study of Billy the Kid in characteristically Freudian 1950s fashion. Paul Newman was Billy, who in the film did not wear a wristwatch. **148.** Originally a child actor on stage and screen, **RICHARD QUINE** found a home for himself at Columbia in the 1950s with a series of light comedies. In *Bell, Book and Candle* (1958) Kim Novak had one of her best comedy roles as an up-to-date Manhattan witch. **149.** One of Hollywood's great musical directors, **VINCENTE MINNELLI** handles a musical interlude in *The Reluctant Debutante* (1958), an otherwise non-dancing M-G-M comedy. Kay Kendall and Rex Harrison practice some "rock and roll" steps, while co-star Sandra Dee is offscreen somewhere with John Saxon.

150

151

152

1902-P13

150. Lana Turner has her own ideas about her role in *Imitation of Life* (1959), to which director **DOUGLAS SIRK** listens politely. This was the last of Sirk's string of Technicolor melodramas for Universal, and his biggest commercial success. Following its release he returned to Germany to work in the theater.   151. A pioneer of East-coast production in the 1950s and 60s, **SIDNEY LUMET** recreated a small Southern town in upstate New York for *The Fugitive Kind* (1959). A child actor who became a successful television director after the war, Lumet has resisted working in Hollywood throughout his career, preferring to film in Europe or New York.   152. Director

ROGER CORMAN (right) and his star, art collector Vincent Price, admire one of the paintings Burt Schonberg has created for Corman's *The House of Usher* (1960). The first of a series of Poe adaptations by the low-budget specialist, *The House of Usher* led the way to a new appreciation of Corman's films, as well as new life for the previously scorned horror genre.   153. Best known for his musicals, especially those with Gene Kelly, **STANLEY DONEN** moved into straight comedies and dramas in the 1960s. *The Grass Is Greener* (1960) was an interesting drawing-room piece starring Deborah Kerr, who like Donen seems lost in thought during a hairdressing break.

154. OTTO PREMINGER was a Viennese theater director whose European film experience was inconsequential. After some success on Broadway he established himself as a producer and director in Hollywood, and even made a mark as an actor—notably in his own *Margin for Error*. Here he prepares a complicated crane shot of Charles Laughton for *Advise and Consent* (1962). **155.** Chroniclers of the M-G-M musical sometimes overlook the name of **CHARLES WALTERS,** from 1947 the director of such solid entertainments as *Easter Parade* and *The Barkleys of Broadway*. Once a dancer and director on Broadway himself, Walters shares a laugh with stage veterans Martha Raye and Jimmy Durante during the shooting of *Billy Rose's Jumbo* in 1962. **156.** A newspaperman turned filmmaker, **SAMUEL FULLER** writes and directs his pictures with the panache of an old-style editor laying down a six-column banner headline. On the set of *Shock Corridor* (1963) Fuller works with Constance Towers, while the headline on the wall reminds viewers of an earlier Fuller classic, *Park Row*. **157. STANLEY KUBRICK** was originally a professional still photographer who entered films with a series of privately financed documentaries. His uncanny use—and manipulation—of "camera realism" has marked many of his finest films, including *Dr. Strangelove* (1964). Here Kubrick consults with Peter Sellers during the shooting of the war-room episodes.

156

157

83

1949-49

158. During the late 1950s and early 60s, **WILLIAM CASTLE** virtually created the subgenre of gimmick horror films, in which inflatable skeletons soared over the heads of audiences and theater seats were wired with electric buzzers. *The Night Walker* (1964) marked an end to all this, however, as Castle tried to find new thrills in the teaming of Barbara Stanwyck and Robert Taylor. **159.** The live television dramas of the 1950s proved fertile breeding ground for a generation of new film directors. **JOHN FRANK-ENHEIMER** spent his years at CBS directing episodes of "Studio One," "Playhouse 90" and other classics of TV's golden age, suitable training for such thoughtful Frankenheimer films as *The Manchurian Candidate* and *Birdman of Alcatraz.* That menacing object is part of a camera crane. **160. ROBERT ALDRICH'S** *The Dirty Dozen* (1967) was said to have inaugurated the wave of high-profile violence in contemporary films. Here even Lee Marvin seems stunned as Aldrich kicks around actor John Cassavetes during rehearsals.

160

162

161. During the 1930s **EDWARD DMYTRYK** worked as an editor, and finally broke into directing with such well-crafted thrillers as *Murder, My Sweet*. The best-known member of the "Hollywood Ten," Dmytryk renounced his earlier political affiliations and was able to resume his career after a brief prison term. He came to New York to film *Mirage* (1965), with Diane Baker and Gregory Peck.   **162.** Relatively few important stars have achieved equal success in directing. **JOHN WAYNE** tried his hand at two spectacular action films, *The Alamo* and *The Green Berets* (1967), with mixed results. Roasted by critics, this latter film eventually proved a moneymaker, despite considerable cost overruns during production.

86

163. PETER BOGDANOVICH moved from writing about films to making them, a transition common in the European cinema, but at the time unprecedented here. With the help of Roger Corman he directed the highly touted *Targets* (1968), in which he and Boris Karloff played an aging horror-film star and his director. **164.** Since Gene Kelly there have been few original dance talents working behind the cameras in Hollywood. **BOB FOSSE** is the prime exception; he moved from energetic solos in films like *Kiss Me Kate* to the interpretive razz-ma-tazz of *All That Jazz*. On *Sweet Charity* (1967), his first as director, Shirley MacLaine was his star.

165. For the shooting of *The Rain People* (1969), **FRANCIS FORD COPPOLA** returned to his alma mater, Hofstra College, and began semi-improvisational shooting with a small crew. Since then his approach has grown increasingly high-tech, but the sense of experimentation with new techniques remains. **166.** Few directorial careers have been as convoluted as that of **JULES DASSIN**, who began with Hollywood *policiers* in the 1940s, rebuilt his career in Europe after the blacklist, and eventually returned to Hollywood to film *Uptight* (1968), a blaxploitation remake of *The Informer*. **167.** The 1960s went out with a wave of high-priced musicals, and one of the last was **JOSHUA LOGAN**'s *Paint Your Wagon* (1969). A significant force in the musical theater, Logan made films that included *South Pacific* and *Camelot*. Lee Marvin (right) gets some help with the music and lyrics. **168.** An occasional director and more frequent actor, **JOHN CASSAVETES** works in both fields with a studied deliberation that delights his fans and confounds his detractors. Like most of the Cassavetes pictures, *Husbands* (1970) was a New York production.

167

168

169. MIKE NICHOLS made a startling film debut with *Who's Afraid of Virginia Woolf?*, an unexpected dramatic success from a man known previously as a stand-up comedian. *Catch 22* (1970) was apparently even more suitable material, but failed to achieve equal success. Did Orson Welles have any suggestions? **170.** As a director **JERRY LEWIS** involves himself in all aspects of the craft, giving special care to the more technical elements. Here with cinematographer Wally Kelley he checks the dailies for *Which Way to the Front?* (1970). Better known as a rather broad comedian, Lewis for a time taught film production at USC. **171.** An independent spirit who has worked with varying degrees of success inside the Hollywood system, **BOB RAPHAELSON**'s best-known film remains *Five Easy Pieces* (1970). Jack Nicholson, who has also written and directed a few films of his own, waits for Raphaelson to finish broadcasting instructions.

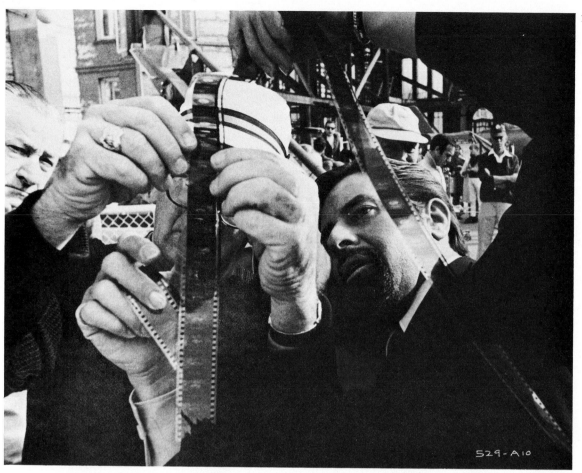

529-A10

172

173

172. One who came up the hard way at RKO, **RICHARD FLEISCHER** represented traditional studio values at a time when film-school graduates with zoom lenses seemed to be taking over the business. *10 Rillington Place* (1971) was a relatively modest Fleischer picture, a respite from *Dr. Doolittle* and *Tora! Tora! Tora!* 173. After a successful career as a producer (including many of Robert Mulligan's films), **ALAN PAKULA** turned to directing in 1969. *Klute* (1971) was a New York location picture starring Jane Fonda, who won her first Academy Award under Pakula's direction. 174. For many, **BLAKE EDWARDS** is the heir to Leo McCarey, a director quite good at dramas, but wonderful at a whole range of comedy. The *Pink Panther* series, *Ten* and *Victor, Victoria* are clear evidence of Edwards' success with a wide range of modern comedy genres. 175. By the 1970s "American" production had become completely internationalized. Polish director **ROMAN POLANSKI**'s *Macbeth* (1971) was filmed in England and qualified as a British production, but the backing came from Hugh Hefner's short-lived Playboy Productions film unit.

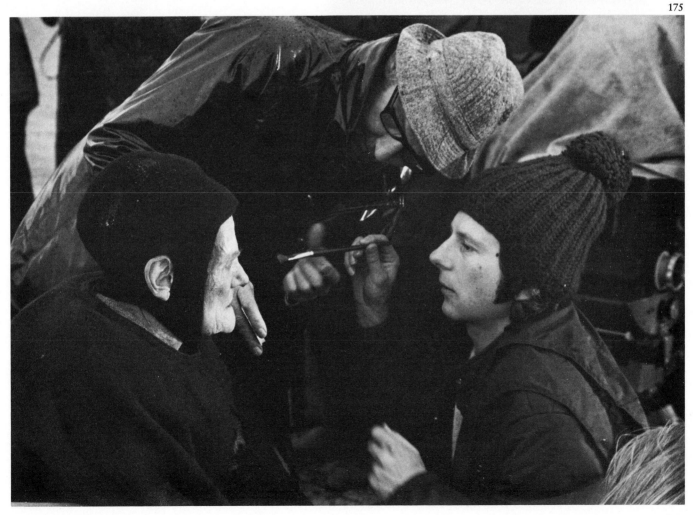

177

176. Best remembered for films like *West Side Story* and *The Sound of Music*, director **ROBERT WISE** is also one of America's top directors of fantasy and science fiction. Since his days with Val Lewton, Wise has handled such classics as *The Day the Earth Stood Still, The Haunting, Star Trek* and *The Andromeda Strain* (1971). **177.** Canadian-born **NORMAN JEWISON** was originally a television producer, and worked on eight Judy Garland shows. His films in the 1960s and 70s were mainly light comedies like *The Russians Are Coming,* and he was the surprise choice to direct the big-budget musical *Fiddler on the Roof* (1971), which starred Topol. **178. ROBERT MULLIGAN** is another New York television director who made the switch to film in the 1950s, one whose pictures reflect that concern with finely observed character development typical of directors trained in this medium. Perhaps his most popular film was *Summer of '42* (1971), shot on the California coast near Fort Bragg. **179. MILOS FORMAN** brought the black humor of his Czech comedies to *Taking Off* (1971), one of the few successful attempts to capture the 1960s cultural revolution on film. One of a growing number of New York directors, he also shot *Hair* and much of *Ragtime* here.

180. *Presbyterian Church Wager* was the working title of *McCabe and Mrs. Miller* (1971), with Julie Christie, one of **ROBERT ALTMAN**'s most interesting excursions into color and design. Among the cinema's great risk takers, Altman makes films that constantly skirt the edge of critical acceptability. Audience reaction is usually unpredictable. **181.** Now the center of the vast *Star Wars* empire, **GEORGE LUCAS** was once a young film-school graduate working as assistant to Francis Ford Coppola. His first feature, *THX-1138* (1971) was an expansion of one of his student films, and starred Donald Pleasence. **182. GEORGE ROY HILL** checks a location setup for *Slaughterhouse Five* (1972), his controversial adaptation of Kurt Vonnegut's novel. A director of Broadway shows and live television dramas, Hill's most successful pictures have been such Hollywood epics as *Butch Cassidy and the Sundance Kid*. **183.** Once a comedy partner of Mike Nichols, **ELAINE MAY** also brought to her work a comic sensibility formed by 1950s improvisational routines. *The Heartbreak Kid* (1972) was the finest of May's few films.

184. One of the most successful of the new breed of independent producers who emerged after World War II, **STANLEY KRAMER** won a new reputation in the 1950s and 60s as a director of such socially significant films as *The Defiant Ones* and *Guess Who's Coming to Dinner?* Gene Hackman starred in Kramer's *Oklahoma Crude* (1973). **185.** The cult director of such Randolph Scott westerns as *Ride Lonesome* and *Comanche Station*, **BUDD BOETTICHER** also had a consuming interest in bullfighting. For over a decade he worked on a biography of his friend Carlos Arruzza, in which he appeared as an actor himself. Avco Embassy finally released *Arruzza* in 1972.

185

186. With *Love and Death* (1975), **WOODY ALLEN** was able to break away from the stand-up comedy mold of his earlier films and tackle a feature-length subject with real dramatic shape and character development. It was the necessary prelude to a later masterwork like *Annie Hall*. **187.** One of our best directors of spectacular action pictures, **FRANKLIN SCHAFFNER**'s films include *Planet of the Apes* and *Patton*. For *Papillon* (1973) Schaffner (with cigar) was able to imbue a vast Devil's Island escape melodrama with the intimacy of an exacting character study.

187

188

189

188. One of the few writer-director-producers constantly active over the past thirty years, **RICHARD BROOKS** effects a control over his projects few recent directors have achieved. He worked with Ian Bannen and Gene Hackman on *Bite the Bullet* (1975), an ambitious western epic. 189. Today's most important star-turned-director must be **CLINT EASTWOOD,** who trained for the job with Don Siegel. In his films as director Eastwood has been able to project his acting persona in an uncanny fashion. 190. **MARTIN RITT** (right) confers with screenwriter Walter Bernstein on the set of *The Front* (1976). The comedy/drama on the blacklist era recalled unhappy events in the careers of both men. With films like *The Molly Maguires* and *Norma Rae*, Ritt is one of the few Hollywood directors still committed to films of social and political concern. 191. Most successful of the Hollywood *wunderkinder*, **STEVEN SPIELBERG** is at his best with tales of high adventure and higher technology. His *Close Encounters of the Third Kind* (1977) was crucial in establishing the dominance of a handful of young directors over the floundering Hollywood industry.

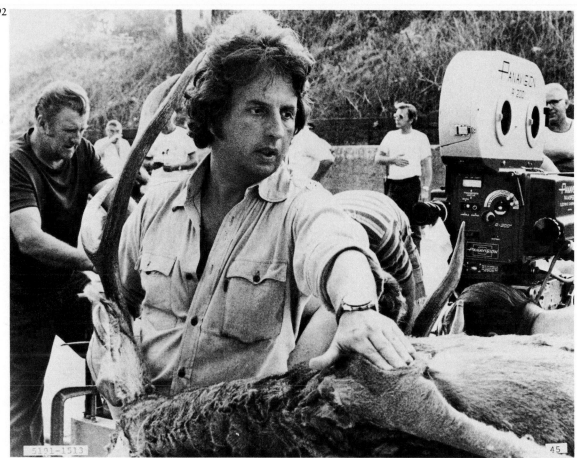

192. A meticulous and painstaking craftsman, **MICHAEL CIMINO** achieved instant fame with the success of *The Deer Hunter* (1978). How this celebrity affected the production of *Heaven's Gate*, Cimino's lavish and languorous western, is one of the classic Hollywood stories of the 1980s. **193.** The one-time apostle of violence in 1970s cinema, **SAM PECKINPAH** (right) cools off during the shooting of *Cross of Iron* (1977) with Vadim Glowna. In pictures like *The Wild Bunch* and *Straw Dogs* Peckinpah introduced an unprecedented level of brutality into Hollywood films. **194. PAUL MAZURSKY** makes intimate films about the romantic dilemmas of modern life, notably *Bob and Carol and Ted and Alice* and *An Unmarried Woman*. His *Willie and Phil* (1980) was an homage to an earlier entry in the genre, François Truffaut's *Jules et Jim*.

195. ROBERT REDFORD won accolades for his direction of *Ordinary People* (1980), with Mary Tyler Moore, but instead of following quickly with another project he temporarily turned his energies away from directing. Today his Sundance Institute is one of the most promising centers for the development of new production talent.   **196. SYDNEY POLLACK** handles the camera himself for a scene in *Absence of Malice* (1981), an act which would have raised eyebrows only a few years earlier. Noted for his close rapport with actors like Robert Redford and Paul Newman, Pollack gives equal weight to the photography and design of his films as well.   **197. MARTIN SCORSESE's** career began at the NYU Film School, hit a peak of Hollywood success with *Alice Doesn't Live Here Anymore,* and now seems to have come home to the mean streets of New York. Working again with Robert De Niro, Scorsese made *King of Comedy* (1982), a chilling essay on the power of modern media.

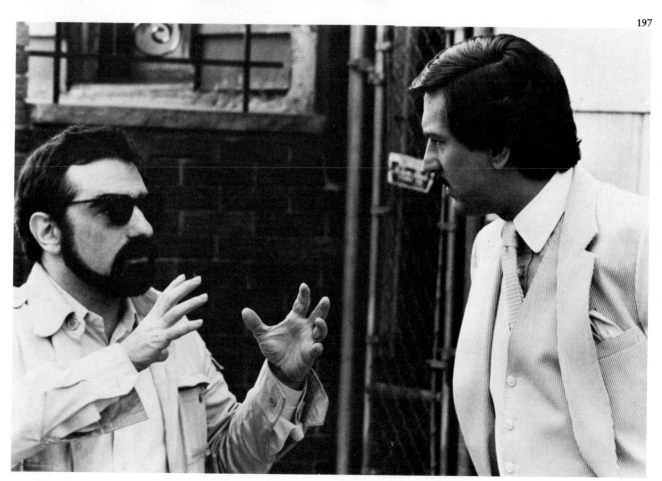

INDEX OF PERSONS

Only persons illustrated are included. The numbers are those of the illustrations.